No ~~Buts~~

by Ryan Buynak

No part of this book may be reproduced without expressed, written consent or permission of the author or publishing entities, except for brief quotes for press or review purposes.

No ~~Buts~~ © 2024 Ryan Buynak
Follow Ryan Buynak on Instagram: @coyoteblood

ISBN: 9798335640930

Cover by icon303
www.icon303.com
Instagram: @icon303

Previous works by Ryan Buynak:

- Yo Quiero Mas Sangre: Random Acts of Poetry
- The Ghost of the Wooden Squid: Random Acts of Poetry
- Montreal on October
- Future Underwater Tomahawk: Random Acts of Poetry
- Sleeping: I'm Just Not Good At It
- Sleeping 2: I'm Still Just Not Good At It
- Writer, Bartender, Skateboarder
- Stolen Days in LA
- Pistol Pantomimes
- Coyote Blood Will Kill/Love You
- A Whole Bag of Hammers
- Hearts & Farts
- Reading Harry Potter in Rehab

"I think perfection is ugly. Somewhere in the things humans make, I want to see scars, failure, disorder, distortion."
— **Yohji Yamamoto**

**Do whatever you have to do
to make your dreams come true.**

Only *Ifs* & *Ands*...

Priorities

Going to an early dinner at 5.
Movie is at 7.
That means I can catch
the end of the Magic game,
and write poetry until midnight.

Time to fix that chainsaw, pal

In a bookstore, looking
for a copy of *Been Down So Long It Looks Like Up to Me*
by Richard Fariña.

I find my own damn books,
snap a photo for the Gram,
and get the hell outta there.

First Playlist of 2024

1. *Bulletproof Weeks* by **Matt Nathanson**
2. *Laundry Pile* by **Arkells**
3. *Difference of Opinion* by **Adam Newling**
4. *Mouth Full of Bones* by **Natalie Portman's Shaved Head**
5. *Gum* by **Moose Blood**
6. *New Comedown* by **Plague Vendor**
7. *Time Shrinks* by **Arcy Drive**
8. *I See It Now* by **Bachelor**

Playing tennis in a tuxedo

Thankful I don't have much to do today;
Whatever I get done is acceptable.

Too sober to talk

I'm at the age where
I am pickling onions
Doing puzzles at
The dining table
And watching shows
About British farmers.

Just Kvetching...

The word "~~but~~" is mostly defensive…

We don't want to render our words used to describe our experience, thoughts, feelings, and reality as insecure and unclear. We also need to deeply reflect upon the words others communicate to us so we can respond from a place of empathy instead of a place of competition to "win" an argument or appear more knowledgeable than others.

Even if you say the word with conviction, confidence, and poise, you are still doing yourself and others a disservice because choosing to say it still exercises the function of negating your previous statement.

Think about it! When someone says, "No offense *but…*", we all know that the next words out of that person's mouth is going to be something offensive.

So, the more we take responsibility for our actions, the less we need the word "~~but~~". And the fewer excuses we have in our lives.

Poem

I don't need a mansion
And a Lambo;
I'd rather live above an old storefront
And drive a beat up pickup

The Magic lost,
The blackberries are moldy
This saltburn flick
Is overrated

I think I healed too much
Because now I don't like anyone
And I feel empowered
To not do anything.

Pace the Cage

I want to reread the old man and the sea
Which I didn't dig when I was teen
Just to see if this me identifies
With the plight of the fisherguy.

Poem

I've made some bad choices in life
Yet I never bought a pair of Crocs.

Don't forget silver

the pink and blue and purple and yellow
sunset
is the romance left behind by the day
mixed with the dreams of the evening
and all of tomorrow's opportunities
before they plummet into the sea of
forever.

iApple

I always buy an apple
Because I tell myself
To eat more apples
Yet I never eat it
And said apple always
Goes to waste.

The Most Dangerous People in the World

Are idiots with ego

Tattoos

My body is decorated
like the notebook
Of a 13 year old
Punk kid in 1996:
Me.

ambulate

I still have Louisville
in my weather app
on my phone.

The Panther Anthem

It don't matter if it rips...

I watched five movies this weekend:
Wonka
Past Lives
Self Reliance
The Prom
Saltburn

Wanna know what January 19th, 2024 feels like?

It feels like this.
If you are reading this—
No matter when or where—
Know that I wrote this
on January 19th, 2024.

Just sitting at the dining table.

(It's almost midnight
So it will be
January 20th, 2024 soon.)

Do you feel it?

I take it all back

I just want to work
On a British farm
And never write again.

I just want a blowjob
And a spliff
And a cup of coffee.

Music is a time machine

I hope the songs I sent you
Still haunt you
In the grocery store
While shopping for spinach.

2006

Making out with chicks.
Listening to Cold War Kids.
Not giving a shit on 86th.
Hoping it never ends.

Seeking solidarity at the end of the internet

When you lay on the floor, stretching,
What's the noise you hear in your head?

The Decaying Corpse of Philip Seymour Hoffman

I'm no epicurean.
I don't need much.
Aside from time.
And peace of mind.

In the era of noodling truth

Ok tea time
And then B time
(Bedtime).

the sword to destiny's neck

my life is like a Barnet Newman
painting.
my strife is like Margarita Engle's
poem about books.

BYOL

Bring your own lasagna
The band doesn't seem to mind
And do the Ligeti lasagna lunge
At the ex of one of your exes

Drumming on the steering wheel with a mechanical pencil

While Linkin Park and Limp Bizkit
Were doing their rap rock shit,
311 was just over here like
We been doing that for like ten years
And we also had reggae in ours!

pareidolia

I met her at the car crash intersection
of youthful optimism and adult precision...

from poetic mornings
to cinematic afternoons
to introspective nights
with indie music soundtrack...

it's all a blur now,
with the cocktail of nostalgia
mixing with the longing of love
and ego and the death of youth...

I see specific moments of the past
pass by in the clouds above me now.

these are the good ol days

confirming Nietzsche's notion
of eternal recurrence,
I stand among the cognoscenti,
having taken a curious tumble
over the past decade or so,
yet I am back and better,
and I got the Magic on,
just ate an edible,
and now eating these insane
Indian chicken wings!

Imponderabilia...

Poem

I wanna be substantial
And stick with you
like an emo song
in the life of a 20-year-old
in florida in 2002.

Little Names & Red Ribbons

We don't have to verbalize our yuck
for someone else's yum.
We can just chew the scenery
with our mouths shut.

seeing windmills as giants

Public standards, a mixed bag they are,
Some reflections are far-reaching, some bizarre.
My identity isn't just a side gig or a play,
It's not something hidden, tucked away.

Let's discuss the highs, the lows in the mix,
Prioritizing life's joys, struggles, the fix.
Setting good examples, shaping our fates,
Liberating others from societal constraints.

Men, women, everyone, let's tear it apart,
The double standards that have played their part.
Break free, be real, let authenticity start,
For we all have lives beyond one single chart.

James Dewitt Yancey's Cadiac Arrest

I am a mix of punk rock
With a little bit of hip hop
And a heart broken by folk.

Alligator Guts

flipped back and forth between the new Beyonce
and the new Idles album today, just to split myself in half,
embrace two of the 6 (hundred and sixty-six) sides of me.

my confidence is reflected in the music I rock:
when I was drunk and morose, it was all sad bastard folk music,
~~but~~ now it is punk and hip hop and soul, baby!

the day job is doing better, the script is coming along,
the rough illustrations for the kids book are drafted in the doc,
the life of a working writer is a barnstormer rollercoaster.

my body is a socialist, because it works for the heart,
my brain is moving faster than before,
and right now Ryan feels good and valued in the universe.

I wish I could make this drug called confidence last,
~~but~~ the wind will shift and the conceit will shift,
~~but~~ I know how to get it and use it now...without excuses.

because seven, eight (ate), nine

I feel good.
Life is good.
Which terrifies me.
Because...

All time is quality time.

I have one main dad rule for myself:
I never say no when she asks me to play #Barbies!

Doesn't matter if I am working or writing my masterpiece.
It's always yes.

And we have our own unique #Barbie universe
with goths and flying babies, where Rosa Parks is the president,
and one character only says "I'm Mark!"

It gets weirder and funnier than you can imagine.

(Side note: My only beef with the #Barbiemovie is in the montage at the end they didn't show one dad playing Barbies!)

Ken and the aforementioned Mark
(whom only says his own name loudly when he speaks
~~but~~ all the other characters can understand him…
kinda like Chewbacca)
are watching #BacktotheFuture in the Barbie Dreamhouse!

#dadlife

I wonder what Sydney Sweeney is self conscious about

I bet it is something that seems silly,
like her knuckles or knees,
~~but~~ then traps her feelings in a box
of not wanting to admit it
because people will be like
"c'mon girl, gimme a break,
you are like perfect,"
in which she responds like
"I am not," so now she is
in a lose-lose situation
where she can't be human
with simple insecurities
because she is beautiful
and people get mad about that.

Tale

Saw Ryan Buynak downtown with his fly down,
hustling among Star Wars nerds towards the tail end
of the pretty good part of the night, vulnerable,
and dimwitted in his fascination with time.

My Whole Life is a Sacrifice

I had to give up my youth.

I had to work my way through high school,
community college, my 20s and so on.

I sacrificed a chunk to lack of confidence.
I gave up a gallon to drinking.

I traded creativity
To make end's meet.

I handed over my life
To my wife and daughter.

Every damn day
Gets dolled out to work.

Every wish is given up
For paying bills and shit.

I'm lucky I have a life to sacrifice.

Re: Poem

Reality is dead
Replaced by a dream world
Reason is poetry
Realness is human interaction

Tuesday CD Listening: John Coltrane's "A Love Supreme"

Sometimes, you need to shut out all the noisy guitars,
raucous drums, pounding bass lines,
and screamy punk vocals for
McCoy Tyner's meandering piano,
sensual bass from Jimmy Garrison,
steady drums from Elvin Jones,
and some smooth saxophone a la Coltrane.

Trivia: This was recorded just a mere seven miles away

from where I am right now in Englewood Cliffs, NJ.

My daydreams are wild in adulthood.

I dream of having friends
that will come over
and watch Seinfeld with me
while making art and drinking coffee.

Who is the father of the baby in Ghostbusters 2?

I have never considered this
Until now, March 22nd, 2024!

Seriously,
They never mention it!

Why didn't they write it so
The baby was Bill Murray's Venkman's kid?

I am 41 years old,
And angry at this thought.

Poem

My grandmother used to lick her finger
To turn the pages of books
And I thought it was so cool,
Much cooler than smoking
And so that is why I like to read.

final drinks at bars where the patrons get a little sentimental with their jukebox money around closing time

My life gets weirder and less relatable the older that I get,
so I try to write in a way that's relatable to anyone with any problem.

Since getting sober, I have made an effort to accept the circumstances of my life for what they are,
and to remain engaged with and curious about them,
even if they don't conform to stereotypes about how writers are supposed to live.

I write puns for ecommerce products for a living,
and then pretend poems for myself,
also asking famous and emerging musicians super silly questions.

All while trying to squash the idea that you have to be completely chaotic
and tortured to make interesting art.

Weltschmerz…

Hundo P(ineneedles)

Eggs with seasoned salt and sage,
The patience of a (bastard) with(out) saint(s),
Mixed with my mother's rage,
Believing in myself with a side of doubt,
Because we are all horrible, wonderful people,
Just trying to figure it (all) out.

Pickleball Poem

Well I played pickleball for the first time,
So does that make me officially old?

It was fun ~~but~~ hard to adjust to
When I am used to the physics of tennis.

I'll be going for third shot drops before ya know it,
And flirting with the old broads on the next court.

I Lived Fast, ~~But~~ Didn't Die Young. Now What?

Just saw a girl in a Chili's
In upstate New York
 wearing an Orlando Magic hat.

If she were attractive
I would've written about her
forever.

~~But~~ she was an uggo
And so I said go Magic
Then Pointed at the Magic hat on my head.

To which she looked baffled
And so I point at her head again
Cuz I thought it weird we have the same team

A Florida basketball team
That the nba doesn't even like
So it feels super niche up here, upstate.

I proceeded to my fajitas
Which were sizzling something good
Yet I couldn't stop thinking of why?

She looked super confused
Like she forgot the hat on her head
Or she was probably not even a Magic fan.

In that case,
Fuck her poser ass
For not repping what she is into.

Like why not freaking rocking
Something you know and like,
Even if that shit is like Nickleback.

Own it, girl,
Own that shit,
Live your best life, Bitch.

Then I thought
What if someone gave her the hat
And it is just sentimental crap.

That's stupid though, I thought,
And touched the fajitas skillet
To see if it was still hot.

And it was still hot,

And they never give you enough cheese,
Yet always give way too much lettuce.

Like I am using only the meat,
The peppers and onions
Cheese and guac, yo!

Fuck pico de gallon,
Am I right?
And fuck paying with an app.

Which is what they encourage
You to do, while if you insist
They will still run your debit card.

They ran mine,
After I said I don't want to
Download a freaking app.

So I paid and left,
And tried not to make eye contact
With the uggo in the Magic hat.

Poem

I want to leave this bar
~~But~~ I paid $10 for 6
Conway Twitty songs
On the Touchtune jukebox.

I Hate Hokas

They look like shoes specifically designed for handicapped people,
And they are not that much more comfortable,
So the compromise of style and function isn't there.

We can go to the freaking moon,
~~But~~ we can't make cool shoes comfortable?

Any shoe that touts being healthy
Or the 'most comfortable'
Are either ugly running shoes
Or bulky old people clogs.

Some assholes may claim to like Hokas,
~~But~~ if given the chance to design their own shoe,
They would never come up with that crap.

Poem

my grandmother used to lick her finger
to turn the pages of Louis L'amour books,
and I thought that was so cool for some reason,
much cooler looking than smoking,
and so that is why I read.

I don't give a shiver…

When I can't remember someone's name
I just call them 'Scribbles'

Regardless of pronouns,
Scribbles just works.

Try it sometime,
Everyone loves it.

circumscribed

no, officer, I wasn't texting and driving...
I was writing poetry about the moon.

Would you tell Picasso to sell his guitars?

skipped the poetry show tonight,
needed some me time.
bought a Louisville hat,
just for the fuck of it.

the microwave is doing that thing
where I put something in it for fifteen minutes
and it's still cold,
~~but~~ then if I nuke it again for 20 seconds,
and it's like lava.

I'm so glad the Star Wars emo nerd subculture exists.
I'm so glad that right now somewhere
a group of middle aged men are playing pick-up basketball
as I reverse blow on this Bagel Bite in my mouth.

going from Modern Baseball to Ariana Grande,
everything reminds me of the past,

~~but~~ nothing reminds of the future,
and I can ask a philosopher about love
or a cardiologist about heartbreak.

be the leader or be led,
~~but~~ find a balance between both those things
where you can just create and disappear
into the day and it's okay.

I am a vulnerable bull
apologizing for being in a China shop.
I see the eyes of the Buddha
telling me to pick who I fail for
and simply follow through.

Risible…

I hate small talk.

I wanna talk atoms. death. aliens. sex. the meaning of life. that feeling when someone you love txts u. Time travel. what morbin shit makes you laugh. Blackwell GPU architecture. ur childhood. what keeps u up at night. I like people with depth. i dont want to know "whats up" or anything to do with real estate or the weather 😉

This is like an Elizabeth Hardwick story.

Where a young woman returns from New York
to her childhood Kentucky home
and discovers the world of difference
within her.

Cookies on the brain? OMG, samesies! Always!

I think about cookies
More than I ever thought
About booze…
Even in my darkest days.

That may not be healthy either,
~~But~~ semi-sweet chocolate chip
Is better than shitty whiskey
And the regrets that follow the latter.

Yellow

Autumn is the best season.
It sleeps on the back of summer.
Relieved to be a thousand hues.

IDK 😔

Spilled keto ice cream on the piano.
Paused the Vampire Weekend.
To concentrate on cleaning up the keys.

Feels like my halah guy was kinda brand new today.
Didn't tell me to take a soda.
Mohammed probably has his own shit going on.

Missed a perfect poem about the human condition.
Love and loss are now just forgetting to remember.

I don't care about the eclipse

Let the moon veil itself in shade,
while I revel in the my life on earth,
For in my daydreams, for what they are worth,
A timeless terrestrial chaos that won't degrade.

Eclipses come and eclipses go,
Yet steadfast shines all that is below,
So why fret over a fleeting show,
When life on earth whispers tales we know?

In shadows deep, my doldrums still creep,
A daily dance, a night's grand might,
~~But~~ I, unmoved by darkness in steep
The stars gaze upon our emitted eternal light.

Solitude rain Friday night

Angeles by Elliot Smith,
an improvised poem and a soda pop.

Thinking about pancakes tomorrow,
and putting too much ~~butter~~ because I can.

A Bukowski book pulled from the kitchen,
flipped to a random page that is perfect...

"and when nobody wakes you up in the morning,
and when nobody waits for you at night,
and when you can do whatever you want.
what do you call it, freedom or loneliness?"

How long ago did the song end?
How long ago did the silence begin?

A heartworming tale

I have no doubt that
In another life
I am dead.

never skip the embodied reference to the foundations that help me believe

I am going to make a country album one day,
~~but~~ it will be all about the neighborhood of Yorkville in Manhattan,
and be drenched in airport beers and the fears of a 30 year old man
who has a plan ~~but~~ doesn't know how to...

All these LinkedIn losers and Instagram idiots
talk about and talk to creatives who have sold a boat load
of books or bullshit about this or that,
~~but~~ they never talk about the upcoming creative
who is carving their art in trees in Central Park
or working three jobs to pay rent and keep creating.

I used to adhere to made-up deadlines because I thought I was going to die,
~~but~~ now I don't do that dance because I am afraid to die,
like once something is done or on the verge of attention,
I will croak and it will be part of Hashem's joke.

Black Violin

A cowboy hat covered in Christmas lights.
An invisible violin coming from somewhere out of sight.
A rainbow at night.

Reading Kafka's diaries by the lake.
Tonia unsent a message.

Shirt on the floor no more.
Radiohead song solidarity.
The third line of this stupid stanza.

The rose holds me.
Thorns dug deep.

Bacon and spray paint > Rising and grinding

From Caitlin Clark to Orlando Magic,
Sunday Afternoons are for basketball.

A belly full of late breakfast of bacon,
Finger tips black and red of spray paint.

I collect on the couch to catch up
on reading and hoops.

Been a long day of writing
And editing in intervals.

Between being a dad
And living a life.

Rising and grinding isn't always

Athletes and asshole Gary V wannabes.

Sometimes rising and grinding is
Bacon and spray paint.

Then driving your kid to acting
And writing dialogue in the parking lot.

ceramicist

In cupboards, we crawl again,
along the edges of chipped tea cups
with old foes never forgotten,
and new friends not yet rotten.

Don't be stupid after easter,
turn and burn and bang out
poverty poems about believing
in seamless dreams of the future.

Let's joke about yesterday,
and never double dare tomorrow,
expel everything you ever thought,
New York feels so cold even when it is hot.

Don't hump while holding a pencil...

Played List

Lonely People by **America**
The Place That Makes Me Happy by **The Moss**
I Got Heaven by **Mannequin Pussy**
This is Life by **Winnetka Bowling League**
Larry David by **Ok Cowgirl**

Chaos Logic

I wish manatees flew
and were as bountiful as birds,
making the world
a little weirder.

Our future flying cars
will navigate no-wake zones
in the air to dodge
the soaring sea cows,
who are still slow and curious.

And there goes
my last alibi
of dreaming
just to dream.

The night John Prine went to Heaven I woke up around 3 in the morning and wrote this poem right quick

I wonder if
for someone
I am the one
who got away?

Cake

I am so sorry
for hurting you.

Back then,
I simply wanted it all.

Now all I want
is time and cake.

Eat plant-based cobra meat with Larry Bird while refusing to believe lacrosse is hard

I wish tears shot put,
sprayed like a squirt gun,
the kind you win
with tickets that the arcade.

I wish tears made a sound
like a leaky faucet,
turned upside down
like Dr. Seuss' nightmares.

I wish tears were cold,
like water from a pink Stanley,
next to a plate of lava-centered Totino's Pizza Rolls
for contrast to tongue.

Poem

The world needs
more poets.

Less "influencers."

Being a dad is awesome, being a parent sucks!

they don't come with an instruction manual.
It's insane.

That's also what I learned from writing—
that this thing we're doing, our wild, chaotic
daily existence, filled with joy and difficulty,
labor and love, is a timeless one.

Parenting is one of those rare experiences
that links us across time, space, and culture,
that connects us in an unbroken chain,
back thousands and thousands of years.

Raising children is the hardest thing you'll ever do.

And I wouldn't trade it for the world.

Poem

All is fair
In comedy
And poetry.

Scorpio Moons

and thinking about someone so much that
you appear in their dreams

and unintentionally receiving information
about people.

and being constantly permeated by the
visceral lived experience of everything.

Poem

When you used to roll
With criminals
And now your anxiety
Goes down
When Gin Blossoms
Comes on at Publix.

eating ice cream in the back of a unitarian church

sunlight filters through stained glass hues.
I sit and savor pistachio/blueberry.
hiding from the rain, forgetting about instinct.
an invisible organ plays hymnals just for me.

unsure if this is prayer, because no one taught me how.
~~but~~ I am hoping Hashem hears my inner monologue.
I don't ask for anything, just say thanks for everything.
lick the spoon and consider the afternoon.

a hobo sleeping in another pew starts snoring.
I hope she is dreaming of her version of Heaven.
while the Epicureans retreat to their gardens.
my Canterbury tales continue to trail forward.

I am a proxy poet to the world I live in.
protagonists don't have to be "likeable."
I don't have cash or coins.
so I sneak Starbucks giftcard near her satchel/pillow.

outside, the Union Square spring air.
mixes songs of nostalgia and future hope.
the Rumbler reminds me to look down.
and I see I have spilled dreams all over myself.

Louisville Ladder

the past, a dead-fly-covered
old iPhone box, filled with cables
I "might use one day."

the present, hot as a coffin
kept in a Florida attic,
will be tossed in the sea soon.

the future, an inveterate autumn,
despite the duct tape,
another name for the past.

time, a paint-splattered ladder
leaning in the cobweb corner,
waiting to be climbed.

Glass Satisfaction

who do you love?
how many books are on your nightstand?
do you miss me?
what's the last music you listened to?
is your satisfaction as fragile as glass?

Just realized Rupi Kaur is hot!

I repeatedly chose fealty
to my own artistic vision
over anyone else's desires.

And I have done so with the clarity
of a man racing against time,
someone who knows that we only get one
go-round,
and tomorrow is never promised.

Humor, secured through trauma,
is the backbone of everything I do,
whether it is a podcast or poems.

Creatively I am motivated by wanting
to make something lasting,
as the ultimate form of human connection
—across time and existence.

RIYL

Anagrams; involuntary punning; metaphysical conceits;
seeing all your friends at once; fistfuls of dirt;
farmer's markets selling hot heartbreak.

Stage diving; helping a stranger; road movies;
stick-and-pokes; pedal steel guitar; Eileen Myles;
tombstone rubbings; eternal recurrence.

Carnal knowledge; biting (consensual);
the first Vampire Weekend album; self-mythology;
books that open with the word "fuck"; the best revenge.

"Why I'm Leaving New York" essays;
the last Vampire Weekend album; self-referentiality;
holding on loosely ~~but~~ not letting go.

Have you ever heard of the serial-position effect?

Slugging poems in a CVS parking lot
with a swig of iced black coffee,
like some sort of dead hipster detective,
when a realization slaps the back of my heart.

I've had a few dreams wreck me,
and a few I never wanted to leave,
~~but~~ we all must wake up.

I should've been a comedian instead of a poet—
different open mics in different basements—
distracted by the arrogance of time
seen from behind my youthful eyes.

Poetry was easier then;
it is harder now.
I wonder if it is because I am happy?

I want to recall lost lists,
and remember the idiosyncrasies—
the bananas and the benign times
in which everything was nothing.

All the secrets of the fine gone world...

ataraxia

I want to be a dumb ditch digger,
~~but~~ I fall in love too easily.

I want to be quiet,
~~but~~ I can't shut the fuck up.

I want to side with Jung,
~~but~~ I don't know if I am confirmation bias.

I want to be happy,
~~but~~ maybe I already am.

I want to be Chet Baker,
~~but~~ I don't have any of the skill or lasting legacy

I want to be still,
~~but~~ I can't stop moving.

From fiction to action.

You create a piece of art and then you start to see it in a context...
a crack in a sidewalk could be not the language in which
this theme is being embodied ~~but~~ the theme itself.
A Choral History of a Piece of Heaven,
soft pastels on black paper and ceramics, solo show in 2023.
We live in a huge sea of images and we don't know what to look at.
All days arrive the same way: ya either wake up or ya don't.
I woke up today, stepped on a crack, wrote this poem.

Galvanized

into the milieu of the pretzel room
with a stubborn DIY ethos,
I'm only interested in
'Possibles' and 'becomings'.

this relationship is harder won,
wrestling with an inherent, libidinal presence,
the tentative, phantom-catching nature
of poetic exploration without villain.

I protect this interior space
while revealing it through torque,
the slope of a declined gaze,
in contrast to self-portraits.

laden with enhanced chromatic intensity,
and time-specific autobiographical detail,
I long abandoned "easel" poetry,
inviting the reader into my subjective environment.

my new strategies of refusal and tension,

along with more spontaneous preparatory techniques
have shifted gesture and form on the page/screen
to conjure presence, in and by the poem itself.

Instagram landmarks that fit a lifetime
of aspirations and daydreams,
instead I will super glue the wound on my thumb
and hitch into the idiosyncratic wilderness of life's
snacks.

death is such a weird thing.

We must slow our clocks,
pay extraordinarily close attention
to the minutes
throughout our day when life seems
to yawn.

We must then attempt to fill our
days
with time-expanding moments;
not rollercoasters of drama or rise-
and-grind bullshit,
~~but~~ of holding hands and changing
plans
so you can keep your feet in the
sand
just one minute longer until the
water reaches your ankles.

We must make death fear life's
little things
because you ARE the Big Bang,
and everything is what you are and
you are everything,
so go live in the mini moments
between milestones,
because those are the miracles.

Stop asking what my tattoos mean!

some summers last so long
that they never end
even before they begin.

what does it mean
to be human
in a world
without meaning?

I have never asked someone
about their tattoos,
just as I have never interrogated the moon
about where is goes at noon.

trust me, it takes a lot to know a man
to understand the warrior,
the wannabe, the sage
the little boy enraged.

some nights are so wise,
and sum of days are so dumb,
because all your joys add up.

Poem

Leg room in our heads,
paring off the edges of the past,
bumper stickers speaking,
cafeteria noise,
dreams dreams dreams.

There is a burial ground under this merry-go-round

I wanna do everything,
~~but~~ I don't want to do anything.

For instance...

I wanna go see Pearl Jam
in Chicago this August,
~~but~~ I don't want to download an app
for the tickets,
book a flight,
book a hotel room.

I just want it
and everything
to happen.

Sheket Bavakasha!

I write the date on a piece of paper—
the upper right corner,
just like my 4th grade teacher taught me—
and gasp at how those year numbers
keep climbing, despite me trying
to reverse the curse of time
and the decay of age.

Put the nails in the pine (you're coming with me)

Sorry I'm late,
I was sitting in my car out front,
finishing "Rain King"
by Counting Crows.

Walt Whitman's Father

The father,
strong, self-sufficient, fair,
funny, thoughtful, kind…

The offered hand,
the word of encouragement,
generosity, the creative mind.

the entire room including the outside

a guard in the midst
of a Laurie Anderson installation,
my head must be killing them.

what is the purpose of panic?

if this isn't over,
the doorway doesn't need shape,
and the weather will never wonder.

wash in D.C. without me, please.

busboys and poets,
Habeas Corpus,
my ceiling is your floor.

only on independence ave.

the garden in the sculptures
are not where they once were,
nothing is.

Cheese of the Weak...

I Fucking Hate Mother's Day

Not because my mother
Was a manic depressive addict
Who is long dead…

Because of the pressure
It puts on everyone,
Especially the Moms.

It doesn't have to be this way.

The world could be so much fairer…

We could take better care of people,
we could make life easier for parents,
we could make it easier to afford a home.

We could make things more color blind,
we could adjust for past evils like slavery and racism.

We could make education a priority,
And healthcare a right.

We could make technological breakthroughs that would help people,
save lives, preserve the environment.

We could update our infrastructure
and actually plan for the future.

...the safety net could be stronger,
The safety net could be *there*.

Poem

I'm socially hip hop,
yet fiscally punk rock.

Horsefly

does your pitty party come with music?
some little finger sandwiches?

differentiating between what we can change
and what we can't.

in the search for the true you,
we will gift touch, find our cure.

like Buckminster Fuller, I seem to be a verb,
summative, full of everything that made me fall in
love.

Georgia O'Keeffe's Hands

in a world that's exhausting and wearying,
I've made a concerted effort to create artistic habits
that are private and I don't share,
online or otherwise.

somethings should just be for you.

I have historically never made consistent money off of my art;
My practice has been very self-directed and self-generated...
therefore super self-rewarding.

I am an unwitting passenger on currents of history
that are infinitely larger than and entirely indifferent toward me,
which hews the closest to how I really feel
about endings or death or life or whatever,
~~but~~ it is all mine, mistakes and all.

The rest of random

I have tried fate,
~~but~~ it grew grey
and looks like a tv
before high definition.

I have resolved
to rely on randomness,
the divine intervention
of the wayward wind.

I will go and grow
whichever way it blows,
even if I am on a sinking ship,
or a decaying parsnip.

I went back for seconds once,
~~but~~ destiny was like old gravy,
all congealed and real,

too gross and gone.

I warn my eyes
~~but~~ each try
I am surprised
when I cry.

transcend the bitter math

I am not sad,
I just need
a caesar salad
with a side of fries...

Embrace the 'And'

Do you ever catch yourself saying things like, "I love that idea, ~~but~~ we need to do it differently?"

As soon as you say the word "~~but~~," the other person immediately forgets the part about you loving the idea. Because you completely invalidated it with the "~~but~~" and everything that came after it. Instead, use "and:" "I love that idea, and I think a slightly different approach would be most effective." Hear the difference?

In her book Bossypants, Tina Fey breaks down the rules of improv. I took one class at UCB, so I know one of those rules is to always say "yes, and…"
This shows respect for what your partner has to say (even if you don't agree), helps you keep an open mind about the act, and invites you to contri~~bute~~ to the conversation by building on the other person's idea or adding your own ideas. Same goes for communicating at work.

How old was Allen Ginsberg when he wrote Howl?

with a secondhand typewriter,
affection for his friends
of a certain time ilk
came forth at 29 years young.

it captured all the starving,
hysterical, naked, kipling
delicatessen philosophers
that paved the way
for me and my mates.

and here I am at almost 42,
having forgotten a lot of people
who have forgotten me,
a luddite of the lost generation,
the hipsters between Gen X
and the millennials.

way down in the golden brown
of the green grass

is where the good stuff lasts;
under the bestsellers
are the best artists.

I hold up a sign
for the poetry of Kendra Jean
while walking through
the Bowery.

Accept the Simple Miracle of Another Morning

There are days when I think to myself,
"Hot damn! Hot damn!"
You know, like, for example, today.
The blue morning sky,
still with pink clouds.
I read Eileen Myles poems
in silence, sipping my coffee,
and simply accept the miracle.

Photos of Glory, Taken at Turtle Park

Fate doesn't much like paths,
she loves horses and chaos.

Fate throws herself forward
to stop the fall.

Fate doesn't much like math,
she loves turtles and mayhem.

Fate drinks
where the bartenders drink.

Fate doesn't much like taking baths,
she loves showers and power.

Poem

lost my sense of irony.
went looking for it.
in the mosh pit.
of an Idles symphony.

Sociology Mongo (fascinated by sub cultures)

Oh, you are a secret champion powerlifter?
I am here for it!

Oh, you play Zelda and go to metal concerts?
I want to know more!

Oh, you're a neurodivergent event planner?
I have so many questions!

Oh, you're a poet with a music podcast?
Tell me more.

the ghost of A.S. Byatt

I upcycle anything cardboard
and turn it into postcards.

Nike shoebox.
Ziplock bag box.
VHS tape cases.

I upcycled my life.

Fatherhood.
Sobriety.
Passion.

I upcycled time, too.

The hunger of the imagination.
My past...continuously.

"No wheezing the juuu-uice!"

I am like a cross between
Conan O'Brien and Larry David.
"Silly and angry," she said,
And I take it as a compliment.

Nostalgia vs Ephemera…

Ben Affleck Summer

slightly stressed.
with an iced coffee.
wearing jeans.

To preen, wander, and soar

I will never let go
of De La Soul.

I will always scan
the sidewalk for treasures.

I will never pass
on Plath.

I will always say yes
to playing Barbies.

I will never not love
getting lost.

we all want someone worth shouting for!

*How many men did I reform
and make into wild yaks?*

*How many hearts have I broken
kicking them out?*

*How many losses have been silenced
because I was living too loud?*

*How many wins have I missed
due to my soul being too quiet?*

*How do I get my tomahawk back?
How do I find love like a heart attack?*

Summer.

Passion Pit weather.
Matt and Kim weather.

...the sun was made for 2010s indie pop.

We all wanted summer.
And now it is a hundred and fuck degrees.

...Be careful what the proverbial we wishes for.

I sweat with the best of them.
Get nostalgic with the worst of them.

...chasing that forgotten first love face.

The petrichor comes.
Washes it away without rain.

Welder Wings

The miracle of life, of existing in this one way train of life. Where you just grow through time. The miracle of change and time. I was all of these different people. My very identity is this ever-changing thing and I'm constantly learning and in awe of life and over time it keeps on developing ~~but~~ no matter where you are at the time, like in the song, "Oh, when I turn twenty-seven then I'll have it all figured out,' ~~but~~ of course you never do.

If you could time travel...

what would you wear?
what would you eat?
where would you sleep?
who would you keep?

LIVE TIRED

I go insane everday
just
so I can maintain...

cuz you got up at 4:45am to do 200 sad dad sit-ups
in a sweltering Florida garage
and then drank celery juice
cuz someone on IG said it is good for you.

cuz you have a hard rule that you never say no
when your daughter asks you to play Barbies
or put on a living room production of Chicago.

cuz in addition to your day job
you are writing a screenplay, a kids book
on top of the twelve books of poetry you have "in the works,"
while also producing a weekly podcast.

cuz you stayed up late laughing
at a new standup special
with the love of your life.

cuz you flew to NYC
just cuz you miss it and can't be away from it

for too long or you lose a piece of your dumb heart
as if it were dependent on a crackhead-covered bench in Union Square.

cuz life is for living,
cuz one day you're gonna die.

...I am a dancer
~~but~~
I can't dance.

…No alligator guts.

I Hate Money

Blah blah blah.
I don't care about it.
Or want to think about it.

I just want to buy my books,
Get a few tattoos.

Give it all to my kid.

e·qua·nim·i·ty

bouncing one of the Four Brahma-viharas
on the basketball court with Kirk.

mornings considered the sublime
or divine abodes of my time.

finding simple solidarity is invaluable,
more than a million three-pointers in a row in the rain.

the world needs more moments
shared between creative people.

less influencers, less Kardashians,
~~but~~ you can never have too many artists.

Driveway Fireworks

In the heart of summer's warm embrace,
Where the evening sky holds a velvet grace,
Families gather with gleeful cheer,
To celebrate freedom's day, drawing near.

On the driveway, simple yet profound,
Crackling sparks leap from the ground.
Tiny fountains of red, white, and blue,
Painting the night in hues anew.

Children's laughter, a sweet serenade,
As fireflies join the parade.
Moments of awe, wide-eyed wonder,
Echoes of joy in the night's thunder.

Smoke curls softly, a fleeting mist,
Kissed by the light of a midsummer tryst.
Sparklers twirl in tiny hands,
Tracing dreams in golden strands.

Neighbors smile, sharing the view,
In these simple moments, bonds renew.
No grand display, no booming might,
Just driveway fireworks, pure delight.

Under the stars, in the warm night air,
We find magic in moments we share.
For in these sparks, our hearts ignite,
The simple beauty of freedom's light.

The difference between lasers and light

A laser generates a beam of very intense light.

The major difference between laser light
and light generated by white light sources (such as a light bulb)
is that laser light is monochromatic, directional and coherent.

Monochromatic means that all of the light
produced by the laser is of a single wavelength.

This is a lot like love in that
we have different types of love focused on
different people in our lives.

Some are feeling lasers.
Some are feeling light.

Political Poem

This is not a time to be dismayed.
This is punk rock time.
This is what Joe Strummer trained you for.

It's time to be a good person.
That means more now than ever.
This is go-time!

Cigars & Root Beer

From podcasting to poetry,
I am shucking and jiving
along this great green summer,
~~but~~ the biggest challenge
is ~~finding~~ making time
to sit down, shut up, and relax.

Power Poem

My superpower is being able
to snatch happiness
from even the darkest times.

My nemesis is
drinking for fun and drinking for misery,
navigating adult friendships, football,
death and dying and sex,
late-stage capitalism...

My weakness is being able
to fall in love
in the most heated moments.

We're all reading Annie Ernaux, so what?

"There is no other way to produce creative work than under arbitrary constraints."
 - *Rachel Connolly*

It's easy to sit around
and complain about the way things are,
~~but~~ if you've got even a tiny amount of power
to change it, you should try to change it.

In My Service Era

This is the part of my life
that is not really about me.

In big and small ways,
as I happily carry heavy burdens,
I am the driver, the muscle,
the provider, the silent stalwart.

Taking notes, take out the trash,
accommodate the schedule
to have your breakfast ready,
fixing the broken lightbulb in the bathroom.

Time that's quality,
measured in grandly rings
with the goal to add some quantity,

weighted in heavy things,
like memories and milestones,
mistakes and moments.

None of it can be replaced too small–
I don't need gifts or thanks, just more minutes:
As simple as fixing a broken Lego tower
or helping her get dressed.

These years are not about me,
and I am honored to serve.

Unflinching, unapologetic, electric, eclectic, especially imperfect, and it holds no defenses, no excuses, no bullshit…

Ryan Buynak's autodidactic **NO BUTS** is a spiritual sequel to his suburban soliloquy, *Hearts & Farts*, comprised of mismatched melodies and tangled textures, all composed without pretense—its grooves contain an unsung masterpiece of ensemble poetics, unedited, equally unsurpassed and overinspired in its stoic practical positivity…all daring you to stop making bullshit excuses, because life is good.

Made in United States
Orlando, FL
12 October 2024

52532085R00098